LITTLE FILES INSIDE MY MIND

Natasha Marie Crumpler

LITTLE FILES INSIDE MY MIND

Natasha Marie Crumpler

Drizbits Publishing LLc
Sebastain Florida, 32976

Drizbits Publishing edition Dec. 2020
For information about special discounts for bulk purchases, please contact Willie L. Sheard of Drizbits Publishing at
willielsheard@drizbits.com

Table of Contents

File I: Ebbs and flows of life

Why I write

Writing poetry is my art
putting on paper
the contents of my heart.
Writing down the deepest parts of my soul
all the feelings I keep inside
that I have never told.
Writing out the things I'd never
have the courage to say
because I know deep down
it's a high price to pay.
Writing out my deepest thoughts
calms all the feelings
I have tangled in knots.
Writing is my art
spilling all the feelings I've
buried deep inside my heart.
Writing is my gift
it's something that I quit
that I have truly missed.
Deep inside I know that writing
is my therapy
it's the only way that I can
give my mind a sense of clarity.

Overthinking

Here I am again
Lost in my thoughts
My mind keeps wandering
I'm feeling distraught.
Jumping to conclusions
The craziness in my head
Thoughts running wild
So many feelings left unsaid.
Please stop the madness
I whisper to myself.
These thoughts are out of control
I'm falling deeper into a black hole.
A hurricane is raging inside my mind
I'm drowning in my thoughts
Feels like I'm frozen in time.
These thoughts are overflowing
Breaking the dam
Why can't I stop these thoughts
Dancing in my head?
Over thinking is my drug
Feelings of dread.
I'm tired of this addiction
Thoughts filling my head.

I can't take this anymore
I just want to feel fine
I no longer want
to be a victim of my mind.

Introvert

Putting pen to paper
is how I express my thoughts
but to say them out loud
it seems I'm at a loss.
It's easier to tell the paper
then to let someone in
how to open up
I don't know where to begin.
I'm the girl who will listen
to all your hopes and dreams
I'll be the biggest cheerleader
you have on your team.
But all my hopes and dreams
I never get the courage to share
I guess I just feel like no one will care.
Being an introvert and growing up shy
it's easier to stay on the sideline

while everyone else passes you by,
because you feel like when you talk
people will get bored
and there is no worse feeling
than being ignored.
So you keep things to yourself
to avoid getting hurt
wondering how it would feel
to be an extrovert.
Saying how you feel without
caring what others think
it's something I can't do so I feel these
pages with this ink,
because my notebook gets me
on the paper I am free
being outspoken I'll probably never be.
I've always been the girl
without much to say
I don't know why I've always been this way.
I'm going to share my thoughts with you
that I have kept within
just promise not to hurt me
when I let you in.

Alone

I don't fit into any crowd
I'm not a part of any cliques
In this life of choices
I'm never anyone's first pick.
If I were a book
I'd be the last one on the shelf
why should anyone choose me
when I don't even choose myself
I don’t open up to people easily

I'm used to being alone.
I guess I'm just completely comfortable being on
my own
how I'm really feeling
no one can ever tell
I keep all my thoughts and feelings hidden behind a
hardened shell.

When I'd open up and give parts of me away
it seems the more I open up
the less people tend to stay.
I let my guard down
just to watch them leave

my mind tells me I'm not good enough
so I start to believe
maybe I'm just too damaged
for anyone to love
it seems my life is so easy
for them to walk out of.
So I keep my guard up
and stay to myself
keep collecting dust
like an antique bookshelf.

All I've ever wanted
was to feel like I belong
but maybe I am just better off
being on my own
because even in a crowded room
I feel all alone.

Behind my smile

I hold all my emotions behind a pretty smile
Keeping all my thoughts together in neat little files.
I walk around pretending everything's okay when
it's not, don't show any emotions keep them tied
into a knot, because every time I let someone get
close they never stay. All the parts of me I shared
they take when they walk away that's why I keep
my feelings bottled up now there's so many it's like
an overflowing cup. Nobody knows sometimes I cry
myself to sleep the trials in my life sometimes hit
me way to deep. Nobody knows that in a crowded
room I feel all alone I feel better one on one or
completely on my own. When people ask me if I'm
okay I say I'm fine opening up to others is going to
take some time but for now I'm just going to keep
my neat little files and keep all my emotions hidden
behind my pretty smile.

Social media

The truth about social media is
no one cares to get to know the real you
what's on the surface is more important
they don't care to break through the altered
reality of life that you show
but who you are really they will never know
let me post a picture showing
all my assets get 500 likes
but post a quote, a poem or how you feel
maybe get 5 likes
when did life become a competition of
who's living better than who
measuring your worth based on how many
likes and how many views
it seems that life has come
down to reposts and shares
constantly comparing your life with theirs
the life they live behind the screen
you will never see
open up your eyes and realize it's not reality.

Rejection

The sting of rejection is just a part of life
the hurt that it brings cuts like a knife
it seems like no matter how hard I fight
things just seem to never go right.
Why don't things ever go the way that I planned?
I don't know how much more I can stand.
I'm tired of doors being slammed in my face
I don't think I'm going to finish this race.
I feel like I should just throw in the towel
I never get a home run all I get is a foul.
I felt like everything
was finally falling into place
but when it comes to my life
that's just never the case.
Right now all I want to do is give up
but I must be strong and hold my head up.
This pain is only temporary
it won't last forever
I have to believe that in time
things will get better.

Curveball

I paint a picture in my mind
of what life is supposed to be
the visions I create just seem so real to me
imagine my disappointment
when I'm snapped back to reality.
Life constantly throws curveballs
I think we all agree
the quicker you accept them
the happier you'll be.
Sometimes we make plans
that just don't work out
obstacles are thrown to make you
take a different route.
At the time it seems as though
your life is falling apart
but change your point of view
and realize it's just a brand-new start.
Take a deep breath
and remember not to stress
because life will throw a curveball
that works out for the best.

Journey of life

Nothing in life that happens
comes to you by chance
all of life's curveballs
are part of a bigger plan
they enhance the beauty of life
not knowing them in advance.
Life is all about taking chances and risks
it seems we fear things ending
before they even begin.
We should learn to love the journey
instead of anticipating what's next
enjoy the little things
that are not so complex.
We only get one shot at this thing called life
so stop being in a hurry
and just enjoy the ride.

Masterpiece

It's taken me many years
to learn to love myself
to not compare my body
to anybody else.
I don't have the hourglass shape the
inflated boobs, injected ass, and tiny waist.
I don't have a build-a-body
I have real woman curves.
I don't look like a model
I'm just an average girl.
I embrace the stretch marks
engraved on my waist,
the rolls that blanket my sides plus
the little dimples that reside on my thighs.
The milky chocolate of my skin
The gap in my front teeth.
It's not what's on the surface
but what lies underneath.
My beauty comes from within
This idea of perfection doesn't have to equate to
being thin.
No matter what anyone else thinks
my worth will not decrease because
I'm a work of art
I'm a masterpiece.

Road to Success

It seems no matter how hard I try
things just don't work out for me
the ocean seas are as rough as they can be

the puzzle pieces don't fit,
the stars don't align
this journey I'm on doesn't
follow a straight line

waiting and waiting
for things to fall into place
wondering if I will ever
run at the right pace

the life I'm chasing
is always just out of reach
roadblocks bring me to a halting screech

I've put in the work
to get the life I feel I've earned
wondering when it will finally be my turn

my journey to success
has been filled with so many obstacles
and jumping through hoops

it's like my life keep running on the same constant loop

it takes me 100 steps
just to get to someone else's one
running a race they've already won

I know we all have our own
burdens to bare
and I know
that our journeys I shouldn't compare

they say you appreciate things more
when they don't come simply
but it's hard to see the forest through the trees
when you can't see clearly.

Teen Mom

As a teen mom I have always felt judged
like a crumbled piece of paper
with a worn eraser smudge.

Growing up with my son
people always think he's my brother
the disapproving looks I get
when I tell them I'm his mother.

Scanning my finger looking for a ring
where I placed a decoy to lessen the sting.

As if a round object
on my finger would ease my heartache
even though he left me
my son was never a mistake.

When you're a teen mom
people tend to write you off
placing you in their box
of statistics that they can just check off.

Having my son young

didn't mean my life was over
it just meant that I would accomplish
my goals a little slower.

While he got to go on and live life
mine went a different direction
sometimes our greatest blessings
come from our biggest rejection.

I may have missed out
on the typical high school things
but none of that compares
to the joy my son brings.

Even though I was young
he changed my life for the better
the love I have for him
goes deeper than anyone can measure.

"Bitter" Baby Mama

I have never been the bitter baby mama even though there's a myriad of reasons why I should I've a been a single mother since birth and best believe me and my son are good.

It all started with a doorbell ringing at 11 at night I opened the door to an interesting sight the first words out of his mouth were "who's the baby dad?" I was so taken aback and shocked.

I couldn't even be mad I responded saying "it's yours" and he said that's not true I told him yes it is the only person I've been with is you being 17 and pregnant I had to grow up fast.

While he got to go on with life mine became a stark contrast I was not just a teen anymore I became a single mother while he moved on to another and another. As my son grew older he would pass in and out of his life the pain that caused cut deeper than a knife. Accusing me of keeping my son away you can't place the blame on me when you're the one who walked away. I've never said anything bad about him I let my son form his own opinion no matter my position there's a lot more I could say to put him on blast but I moved on and let those feelings pass so no I am not anyone's bitter baby mama but one things for sure I am a child's mother.

File II: Hurt to Healed

Lost

How did I get here?
I lost myself in you
Anything and everything I did it for you.
Putting you first, leaving me last
I filled you to the brim
While I'm an empty glass.
I was so busy holding you together
I didn't see myself falling apart.
It seems as though all you gave me was
another broken heart.
You're shining like a diamond
I'm dull like tarnished jewelry.
Why did I hold on so long?
I guess I was addicted to your foolery.
I finally realized how dangerous
you were to my health
So I'll take the love I gave to
you and give it to myself.

Numb

All I feel is numb
You walked away, you left me
To these feelings I won't succumb
It hurt me to the core to hear you say
we should break up
You wounded me so deeply
Now my guard has gone back up
The damage you caused has taken its toll
I feel no more emotions
My heart has turned stone cold
I gave you all the best parts of me
How could I have been so dumb
I try and try so hard to feel
But all I feel is numb.

Forget the hurt

They say time heals all wounds
To me that is a lie
Trying to forget the hurt
It seems all I do is cry.
He took my heart and soul
and trampled them in the dirt.
I try and try to force myself
to just forget the hurt.
I pick the broken pieces
of my heart up from the dirt
no matter how I try to mend it
I can't forget the hurt.
Inside all I feel is pain
they say you cannot grow or heal
without a little rain.
I wish that I could just forget
and take away the pain

it hurts so much

it feels like I've been run over by a train.

All I have left

are empty promises and scars

you etched into my heart

No matter how much I try to mend

I just keep falling apart.

Letting Go

Sometimes holding on
does more damage than letting go.
I never knew how true this was
til I decided to let him go.
For years I held on to him
hoping he would change
but instead he used my heart
as target practice like
he's at the shooting range.
I made him my priority
while he treated me like a choice.
I didn't realize until now
that I had lost my voice.
In him I had lost my identity
I measured my self-worth
by his infidelity.
Every time he'd beg my forgiveness

and ask for another chance
but this time I will not bend
I'll be firm in my stance.
Suddenly it all clicked
my feelings for him are gone.
My entire life changed
the second I said I was done.
It's like a 10,000 lb. weight
was lifted from my chest
I could finally breathe again
over him I would no longer stress.
I was suffocating under this guise
that he called love.
It's like he had me bound in chains
I couldn't break free of.
All I have is nine years of time wasted
my heart he definitely obliterated.
The biggest lesson of my life
turned out to be my greatest blessing

because I found my worth.

I deserve to be treated like a queen!

What comes next for me

remains to be unseen.

I'm ready to move on

it’s time for me to grow

I'm the happiest I've ever been

since I decided to let him go.

Not a loss

I was the type of girl
who held on to things too long
thinking that in time things would change
but boy was I so wrong.
Deep inside I knew that
it didn't feel quite right
the more I would get hurt
seems I'd hold on extra tight.
I lost so much of myself
in steadily holding on
I didn't want to release my grip
even though he was already gone.
Sometimes people come into your life
who are never meant to stay
when their time is up
I must learn to walk away.
My future will never be tied

to anyone who left.

Even though it hurts

I'm getting stronger with each breath.

What I was fighting for

just wasn't worth the cost.

I finally learned the lesson

that not everyone you lose has to be a loss.

Starting over

I was at a crossroads not knowing which one to take making the wrong choice would be a dire mistake. Should I go right or left I just wasn't sure if I chose left I knew the pain I would endure. Taking that road would lead to a terrible end I would never become a wife just a forever girlfriend. It would be a life of constant emotional abuse there'd be no physical signs like scars or a bruise, but inside my heart would be cold and dying reduced to a life filled with nothing but crying. Thinking long and hard about what I would lose I knew that very moment which one I would choose. I choose to go right have a brand-new start all the hurt and pain I had to depart. I had finally realized what I was worth I'm a precious jewel you'll find buried deep within the earth. I have been renewed like the first signs of spring ready to see what this new journey will bring. I let go of all the hurt and pain I finally found some closure I learned there's nothing wrong with wanting to start over.

He Thought I'd never leave

I fell in love with his mouth
for they told me such sweet words
ignoring the red flags
focusing only on what I heard.
I never realized
that he had me mesmerized
hypnotizing me with the sparkle in his eyes.
Telling me all the things
he thought I wanted to hear.
The words I love you
were like music to my ears,
but words are just empty promises
when the actions don't match.
Creating this nagging feeling
like an itch you can't scratch.
Knowing deep inside

that something was wrong
constantly asking myself
was he just stringing me along.
When he was away
I'd get this suspicion something wasn't right
the saying is true what's done in the dark
always comes to light.
Calling him out
when I'd see him moving shady
then he'd turn it around
on me saying I was crazy.
A woman's intuition
is never ever wrong
and I had ignored mine
for far too long.
To hear me say I was done
the depths of his mind could not conceive
he thought I'd always be there
and that I'd never leave.

We Weren't Meant to Be

I scrolled past your post the other day and
for a second my heart skipped a beat
the memories I have of you
are now all bittersweet.
I thought to myself maybe I still care
but to be honest with you
my feelings just aren't there.
I don't think that you understand
or have the slightest clue
all the tears I cried and years it took
to get over you.
It took me a while to realize
before you left you were already gone
and it hurt that it was so easy
for you to just move on.
But now I look back

and realize it was a blessing in disguise
I'd rather be hurt by the truth
than to be comforted by your lies.
Things I used to beg you to do with me
you do so easily for her
and I don't get what makes her so different
than how we were.
To simply post a pic of us
was like literally pulling teeth
all I could do was sit back
silently seethe.
In your life I was always
at the bottom of your list
you never put me first
I felt so easily dismissed.
Then to top it off
I'd have to beg you to spend time
but now it all adds up
you were never really all mine.

It took some time to open up my eyes

and see that when it comes to you and me

we just weren't meant to be.

Lesson Learned

If I ever find myself in another relationship
I have a list of things I'll never do
never love a man more than he loves you,
never give a man more than he gives you,
don't spend years of your life
waiting for him to make you a wife
you'll wind up years later with nothing to
show but a heart full of knives.
All those years of building him up
watering him so he could grow,
grow into the man I knew he could be
just to watch him turn around and give that
love to someone who wasn't me.
Years upon years he cheated
yet I still stuck around
I guess that makes me boo boo the fool
or bozo the clown.

I guess I have myself to blame

for letting you waste my time

you were so busy chasing pennies

you didn't realize you caught a dime.

You used my heart as if it were

a piece of meat to carve

if this is the kind of love you bring

to the table then baby I'd rather starve.

Looking back years later

I'm glad I made my retreat

I can't let what a man brings to the table

be all I have to eat!

File III: Love to Self-Love

What If

What if you could go back
turn back the hands of time
a second chance a do over
If only just one time.
You can't predict the future
you cannot change the past
maybe it's too late
sometimes feelings just don’t last.
Looking back at life
wishing you had taken a chance
hindsight is 20/20
wish I'd known this in advance.
Now all these what if questions
slow dance in my head.
I didn't have the courage then
I chose to flee instead.
Every time we talk

I swear it feels just like old times

I wonder what would have happened

if I had changed my mind.

I want a second chance

but I'll just hold my feelings in.

I can't believe I just missed

my opportunity again.

Second Chance

After all these years have passed
I can't believe you're in my face.
Who'd have known back then
We'd end up in this place.
They say timing is everything
That much I believe is true.
Even after all this time
My feelings never changed for you.
Whenever we're together
I can just be myself.
I never have to pretend to be anybody else.
I don't know what it is about you
But no one else can compare.
No matter how much we fight It
Our chemistry is rare.
I feel this could be worth it
This time it seems so perfect.

I must admit I'm scared to take this fall

But I'm willing to take a chance

And risk giving you my all.

In Like

Liking someone is scary
not knowing if they feel the same
your minds constantly going crazy
you don't want to play this game.
Every time you think of them
your heart pounds in your chest
the butterflies in your stomach
just won't give it a rest.
Letting your guard down
letting them in
knowing deep down you're scared
to get your heart broken again.
It's a risk you take if you let yourself fall
trusting them not to hurt you
if you give them your all.
Battling with yourself
to let your feelings out

the moment you get the courage

your mind gets filled with doubt.

You have to take the risk

you have to take a chance

because it's better to know

than to always wonder what could've

been.

Competition

Even though I may like you a lot
If I have to be in a competition
Then she can have my spot.
I'm not going to chase you
I'm too old for childish games
All the feelings I felt for you
just went up in flames.
Don't come in my life
If you're going to waste my time.
You're so busy chasing pennies
You can't see that I'm a dime.
When it comes to other girls
it seems that you have plenty
But I'm not the type of girl
to be your one of many.

Games

Please don't play with my feelings
don't play with my heart.
I feel like a pawn in your game
don't make me play that part.
Why do I attract the men
who always waste my time?
Who take me as a joke
and fill my head with lies.
They use me up take their fill
then throw me to the side
I feel like a garbage can swarming with flies.
I've been hurt so many times
it's time to change the plot.
Guys always make you feel
like it's something when it's not.
Now I'm going to change the way that I act
this time I'm going to join the game
you won't like how I play back.

Bond

Imagine having a bond with someone
time could never break
no matter how much time has passed
feels like they've never gone away.
Imagine someone supporting you
in everything you do
but it's not one-sided
because you support them too.
Imagine having someone
who lifts you up when you're feeling down
the encouragement they give you
when you have a breakdown.
Imagine having someone
when they hold you; you feel safe
nothing and no one
could ever take their place.
Imagine having someone

treat you like a queen

on a bad day on their shoulder you can lean.

Creating lasting memories

that will never ever fade

finally getting all the things

for which you have prayed.

They cured your broken heart

and caused it to mend

not only are they your lover

but also your best friend.

The One

I'll be your peace after a long day
I'll be the one to listen
to what you have to say
I'll be the one to support you
help you fulfill your dreams
I'll be the one to encourage you
every step of the way
I'll be the one who's your number one fan
I'll be your backbone
when you feel you can't stand
I'll always be there
to offer you a helping hand
I want to be the one to pick
you up when you fall
I'll build you back up
until you feel ten feet tall
I'll be there to hold you

when life falls apart

I'll be the one to mend your broken heart

I promise

to never take your love for granted

even when things don't go

the way that we planned it

I'll be a ray of sunshine on a cloudy day

I'll be the one to never walk away

I'll be here for you

until the very end

I want to be the one who's

your lover and best friend.

When I start to feel

When I start to feel
I feel way too much
I tend to hold on to my emotions
like a crutch
I'm scared to let anyone get too close
especially the one that I want the most
Every time I let someone in
they never stay
I guess that's why it's easier
to push everyone away
I feel like my guard is slowly tumbling down
I'm getting in too deep I think I might drown
I know I should just
keep him at arm's length
to get my heart broken again
I just don't have the strength
I need to take a minute

to collect my thoughts
I feel like my stomach
is tangled in knots
maybe I shouldn't have let myself feel
I should've given myself more time to heal
I fell too fast I didn't wait
my feelings are so strong
now it's much too late.

Quick Change

I don't know what happened
Things changed over night
I get this eerie feeling
that somethings not right

Was it something I did
or something I said
I feel like all your doing
is playing games with my head

You used to love to talk to me
Now you take hours to reply
Then when I confront you
All you do is lie

We used to be inseparable
Now we spend more time apart
I know it's inevitable
I'll end up with a broken heart

I feel the vibe is off
Your energy is dry
I'm not going to beg you
I'm not even going to try

It's clear as day to me by

the funny way you act
No need to say another word
I'll gladly fall back.

Happiness

If you're only happy because of a man
Honey
reevaluate and change your game plan.
All you're going to get is hurt and confused
Nothing else matters
because with them you are consumed.
Every little thing they do
will affect your mood.
When you get upset
they say you have an attitude.
Emotions going up and down
on a roller-coaster ride.
All the effort you put in you realize
he hasn't even tried.
It's a constant battle
that you will never win
until you learn true happiness

comes from within.

Ladies learn to love yourself

and be your biggest fan

Don’t let all your happiness

be found in a man.

Can't love someone

You can't love someone into loving you
your love won't make them stay
if someone wants to leave you
then let them walk away.
At the time it hurts and despite
what you believe
the person who is meant for you
will never want to leave.
When it comes to love
it seems I get the short end of the stick
I guess I sabotage myself
with the type of men I pick.
I tend to pick the men who always
treat me wrong
but instead of leaving
I stay way too long.
Searching for someone

to fill the empty spaces

so I look for love in all the wrong places.

I'm not going to look for love anymore

I'll let it find me

knowing that in time

what's meant to be will be.

My king will come and find me

show me a love I've never known

so I'll continue patiently waiting

a queen upon her throne.

No Actions

I'm so tired of men
who say one thing then do another
their words and their actions never match
treating you like an option
when you're the ultimate catch
they always gas your head up
with a bunch of bullsh*t lies
they do it so nonchalantly
looking dead into your eyes
to them it's all a game
playing with your head
they're just trying to see
how many women they can bed
well I ain't that woman
so listen up and hear me clear
don't even think to step to me
if you aren't being sincere

your words do not move me boy
if you really want me
your actions better prove it to me boy
because I am not the woman
that you're going to toy around
your true feelings for me
you better break them down
because if you think I'm gonna play games
with you and sit and wait around
boy you must be tripping you're not the
only one who wants me now
if you really want me you
better snatch me up quick
honey I'm the magician
I'll make you disappear like a trick

2 A.M.

It's 2 a.m. I'm staring at the ceiling
my thoughts will not unwind.
I can't escape these feelings
I can't get him off my mind.
Memories of him are etched into my brain
like a permanent tattoo.
Sometimes I lay and wonder
if I cross his mind too.
I've been here before
this feels like déjà vu.
I'm not sure where to go from here
not the slightest clue.
All this time has passed
we picked up right where we left off
feelings that I thought were gone
I can't seem to turn them off.
Maybe this time is different

even though everything feels the same.

Maybe we were meant to reunite

like a moth does to a flame.

In the past it seems like

we always had bad timing

but you never know what can happen

next if you don’t keep trying.

This time I'll put everything on the line

without any fear

because this time

I'm going to make my feelings very clear.

11:11

I lay wide awake as my heart breaks in two
As much as I want to forget
my thoughts always go to you.
I hold in my feelings
I don't dare say them out loud.
I just keep them to myself keep my head
buried deep within the clouds.
The fantasy I created in my head
is better than reality
because deep down I know
your girl I'll never be.
I'll just settle for being
your girl only in my dreams.
Trying to stay silent
as my tears steadily stream.
I stare at the ceiling all I can do is reminisce
look at the clock 11:11 if only just one wish.

Maybe it's better this way

to keep my feelings unknown

because you can't get your heart broken

when your all alone.

Caught feelings

It's far too late
I have definitely messed up
I'm in a permanent daydream
from which I can't wake up.
I let myself catch feelings
now I'm just out of luck
my heart constantly feels like
it's being run over by a truck.
I didn't mean for my feelings
to run so deep
I'm standing on the edge of a cliff
the fall is much too steep.
I told myself from the beginning
to not get too attached
now it's all my fault
from these feelings I can't detach.
Feelings from the past

that have become new

I swear I get this eerie feeling

this sense of déjà vu.

I tried to spill my guts before,

but I was scared how he'd react

because once you say the words out loud

you cannot take them back.

Deep inside you know

that they might not the feel the same

so why bring your heart

any unnecessary pain.

I cannot believe

that I did this to myself again

now with all of these feelings

I can no longer pretend.

It really sucks for me I

know this feeling far too well

so I know my true feelings

I'll probably never tell.

When you like someone

it's like your heart is pierced and bleeding

so my word of advice to you

is to never catch feelings.

Overanalyze

I hate that I over-analyze
and can't collect my thoughts
they form this giant rope
that's tangled up in knots.
All these feelings
hit me in the middle of the night
as my mind goes crazy
I hug my pillow extra tight.
My mind starts telling me
that I'm just too much for you
and you'll never care as much for me
as I do for you.
I go over and over the conversations
for all of them I have reread
then I overthink about what I should or
shouldn't have said.
My heart pounds in my chest

I believe my thoughts are true
I wish I could turn my feelings off
but that's something I can't do.
So I lay wide awake as my thoughts break
my heart in two
it's a sad reality that I've become used to.
In my mind a text is never just a text
I'll lay awake for hours overthinking
now I'm a mess.
In my mind a call is never just a call
because once I start to care
I'll risk giving you my all.
I put my feelings out there
and open up to you
inside my mind keeps telling me
are you sure that's what you want to do.
Between my heart and mind
there's a disconnect
I'm tired of feeling hurt

when things don't go the way that I expect.

Looking at the clock it's 3 a.m.

I realize that I still have more hours

to over-analyze.

Bad Timing

They say the cruelest joke
life will ever play on you
is letting you meet the right person
at the wrong time
unfortunately for me this is true.
So many years had passed
you hit me up out of the blue
feelings you had for me back then
I wish that I knew
because if I'm being honest
I was in love with you.
Being so young I was so scared
it wouldn't work
and the last thing I wanted
was for either of us to get hurt
but life is too short to not say how you feel
so I took a chance and told you that my

feelings for you are real.

I thought maybe this time we could have

a second chance

but I guess an "us"

is just not part of the plans.

The thing about life

is that it's never really fair

and finding the right timing

is maybe just too rare.

I've learned these last few years

if you have real feelings

it’s better not to wait

because the thing about second chances

is sometimes it's just too late.

To say I'm not heartbroken

I'd definitely be lying

I guess when it comes to you and I

we'll always be bad timing.

Spill

I tried to write a poem
to describe how you make me feel
but I couldn't find the right words
no metaphors of butterflies
or singing songbirds
no perfect masterpiece
or a beautiful work of art
so I guess I'll just speak
straight from my heart
I don't have any intricate speech planned
so I'll let the words simply flow
through my hands
you came back into my life
as if you never left
and I think it's time I finally
get this off my chest
back in the day

you were my very best friend

now that you're back

I feel 20 years old again

I was so scared back then to tell you I'd

fallen in love with you

even though we were young I knew my

feelings for you were true

you see to me it just wasn't about the sex

the relationship we shared

was much more complex

we told each other everything

the good and the bad

you knew exactly what to do

to cheer me up whenever I was sad

I tried so hard to hide how I feel

but my feelings I can no longer conceal

I want so much for us to end up together

because life with you is so much better

Words Unsaid

He asked why I looked so serious
I said I didn't know
but honestly my mind takes me places
I'm not sure he's willing to go.
Maybe my eyes speak louder words
than my mouth will ever tell
the closer we get I feel the cracks
breaking in my shell.
Every time he's around
my heart practically beats out of my chest
and the butterflies in my stomach
just won't give it a rest.
I admit because of my past
I'm always on high alert.
I've built a wall so high to avoid getting hurt
but piece by piece
this wall is crashing down.

You've made me want to trust again
and I'll admit I don't know how
the ice I've had around my heart
is all but melted now.
A second chance for us
it seems is now far too late
I should've spoken up before
I guess that's my mistake.
I let my fear get in the way
I thought I'd have more time
maybe we'll reconnect again
in another lifetime.

Unfinished Business

Time is a funny thing described as perfect,
bad, right, or wrong
Maybe time decides that
two people don't belong
but in my heart I don't believe that's true
because no amount of time or distance
will change the way I feel for you
I loved you then I love you still and I know
things change but this never will
I guess my biggest regret
is leaving those words unsaid
visions of us constantly replay in my head
the history we share will never be erased
and as my best friend
you'll never be replaced
I know I can't be selfish
and tell you not to go

the feelings I have for you go deeper
than you'll ever know
I wish I could go back in time
and tell you how I felt
but maybe in this game of life you can't
change the hand your dealt
I guess there's no such thing
as a second chance
maybe it could've worked
under a different circumstance
in the back of mind
I'm still holding on to hope
letting you go this time
I'm not sure how I'll cope
I suppose I have to add a page to my book
of lessons learned
opening up your heart to love means
sometimes you will get burned

Another Goodbye

I've done it again
made the fatal mistake
it seems all I seem to do
is cause my own heartbreak.
Feelings reignited that
I thought were all gone
hoping this time that
I wouldn't be wrong.
When it comes to second chances
I never get any
but when it comes to heart ache
I've certainly had many.
I fall for men who always see me as a friend
but I thought this time
we would have a different end.
I put all my eggs into the basket of him
even though I knew
a second chance with him was slim.
When it comes to me and him
we've always had a great connection
unbeknownst to him he
was the object of my affection.
Even though I didn't mean to

he made it easy to fall in love.
So many nights I prayed to the Lord above
that if he wasn't here to stay
please don't let me catch feelings
because losing him again
my heart can't take another beating.
I guess I'm just angry
at finding myself here again
another broken heart
that I'm left here to mend.
Trying to hold back the tears
I so desperately want to cry
I guess it's time I prepare myself
for another goodbye.

Let Him Go

This time it's going to take a while
for my heart to heal
once again I hid my feelings
and didn't tell him how I feel.
I missed my opportunity
and waited too long
now I'll never get the chance
he's already long gone.
Trying to find the words
for the feelings I couldn't express
now I'm just left here
with a heart full of regret.
In my mind I thought it could work
I guess I'm just destined
to feel nothing but hurt.
It wasn't supposed to be this way
and as much as I want him

I can't beg him to stay.
He deserves to go off and live his life
this hurt I feel cuts deeper than any knife
why it couldn’t be us I will never understand
the life I built in my head
didn’t go as planned.
I'm just left to spill my feelings
on paper to help me to cope
its time I let go of the last bit of hope.
In my life he played a huge part
and no matter where he goes I'll always
hold him deep in my heart.
It's going to take a long time
to gain my composure
I know he's someone I'll never get over.

How do I forget

I'm not sure how to let go
I'm not sure how to forget
all the memories we created
and the time that we spent
was it all for nothing
was it just a waste of time
I'm not sure how I'm ever
going to get you off my mind
maybe I shouldn't have read the message
should've never replied
my heart wouldn't be broken
I wouldn't be losing my mind
I thought maybe this time it would be
different cause we're older
but how can I expect him to wait
around til my life's in order
in the back of my mind I'm still holding on

to hope it will all work out someday

and I'm just disappointed

that it has to end this way

they say I'll get over you

my heart will heal in time

tell me how do I grieve the loss of someone

who was never really mine

Unrequited Love

I want to be the one you wake up to
and fall asleep with every night
I want to kiss your sweet soft lips
and hug you extra tight.
Laying in your arms my back you caress
kisses on my forehead
my head on your chest.
I miss our conversations
in a parked car late at night
from the mundane things to life advice
you always give me a new insight.
The mental connection we share
is intimacy at its best
it's like seeing me naked
without getting undressed.
No one else knows
some of the things I have shared

reconnecting with you
my heart you repaired.
I looked at you as my best friend
until feelings started to creep in
and memories flooded back making me
feel 20 years old again.
When we are together
the butterflies in my stomach do flips
and the words I love you
almost escape from my lips.
The way you look at me sometimes
I wonder if you feel it too.
I hope one day you'll tell me you do
but for now I'll hold this secret in
I guess I'll never know
but if you give me the chance
I promise not to let you go.

Chasing Love

I've recently come to the conclusion
I've been wasting my own time
chasing after love was like
committing the perfect crime.
Falling for men who always do me wrong
that do just enough to keep me hanging on.
So many years wasted
begging and pleading for them to stay
I just couldn't muster the strength
to get up and walk away.
My self-esteem so low
I didn't think I deserved better
settling for those
who showed little to no effort.
What was I thinking
forgetting I'm the one who's the prize?
I guess I just got caught up believing

all of their lies.

Looking back years later

I realized when all of this began

losing my dad so young

I craved attention from any man.

It wasn't his fault he didn't get to stay

so many nights I cried

wishing he hadn't passed away.

A father is a girl's first definition of love

maybe that is why I'll

never find my true love.

It's time I give up I am throwing in the towel

my eyes are wide open

I'm no longer in denial.

So as I raise my eyes

and look to the sky above

I've come to the conclusion

I just can't keep chasing love.

File IV: In my skin

Act white

When I started middle school
I I was told I "act white"
that I didn't act black,
was stuck up and uptight.
I chose to take the high road
instead of resulting to low blows
how they came to those conclusions
I guess I'll never know.
The funny part is I was told that
by people my same color.
Their words cut me like a knife
and they liked to watch me suffer.
I guess I act white
because I don't roll my neck
and clap my hands when I speak.
People take my kindness
and confuse it with being weak.

Supposedly I'm stuck up

since my hair was long

it had to be fake

they'd take their hands through my hair

as if it were a rake.

Trying to find the tracks

that just weren't there

as if I was the only black girl with long hair.

I don’t understand how someone acts white

and because I was smart

I couldn’t be black and bright.

Who knew it would be so hard to be

accepted by my people?

They treated me as an enemy

instead of their equal.

Same Energy

Black women shouldn't be raped, abused, or killed for telling a man no. We're allowed to not be interested without stroking your ego. Learn to take the rejection in stride and not call it disrespect. When you approach a woman you need to learn to come correct. Maybe your mama didn't teach you how to treat a lady, but our names are not "ay ma", "yo shorty" or "come here baby". When we turn you down there's no need to resort to derogatory names for your quick change in demeanor you should be ashamed. We're not on this earth just to fulfill your need for sex treating us as if we're just another box to check. They say black women are fighting three pandemics I admit I have to agree we're out here fighting for men who don't keep that same energy.

Dark Skin Girl

You're pretty for a dark skin girl
I'm not sure what that means
all this chocolate goodness
comes straight from my genes.
The same genes that gave birth
to you as well
if that's supposed to be a compliment
I surely couldn't tell.
Telling me I'm different
and I don't act too black
it seems you have some baggage
I'm not willing to unpack.
Back in the day
I didn't have the highest self-esteem
but the woman I am today
is not someone you're not going to demean.
You say you prefer

to date someone who's white
clearly I'm black
so you must not be too bright.
It's okay to have a preference
without tearing down your own race
I can't believe you had the audacity
to say that to my face.
Honestly, I guess I shouldn't be surprised
its's only so long the self-hate
can be disguised.
They go for the exotic girls
to feel like they are scoring
so they diss their own
to cop the girl who's foreign.

I Am Not My Ancestors

I am not my ancestors
your hate I will not take
when you disrespect me
you've made a dire mistake.
When it comes to injustice
I will not hesitate to speak up
I will not sit back and cower
and will certainly not shut up.
You spew your hate
and try to cover it up with bible verses
and your first amendment rights,
but see the Bible is something
you just can't rewrite.
Nowhere in the good book
does it say to judge and hate
whichever way you try to flip it
this is not up for debate.

To the injustices of people of color
you choose to be blind
but then say all lives matter
to give you a peace of mind.
Just because we're friends
I won't cut you any slack
you can't rewrite the narrative
every time the victim is black.
Disparaging their character with old
mugshots on the news
over and over again
the hate continues to spew.
Then they try to justify
that their actions were right
but we all know the story's different
when the victim is white.
Just because our skin is black
we're no different from you
maybe you forgot that we're still human too.

It's time to open up your eyes and realize

that having black skin

is not something you should despise.

This world could be in such a better place

if everyone promoted what they love

instead of bashing what they hate.

2020

How can it be that in 2020 we still have black bodies hanging from trees viewing us as threats even when we are on our knees. Unarmed men and women killed by police brutality. Black skin is not a weapon it's time to change that mentality. How many more lives do we have to lose before we see a change? It's like open season on us our lives aren't a shooting range. From our friends a deafening silence but hella loud about the violence crying over buildings and statues, but never the lost lives it seems they'd rather watch a black man die in the street than to see a black man thrive. They have the nerve to act like we don't have the right to be mad when all we want is justice not revenge they should be glad. You don't get to tell black people how to be mad when you have the privilege of learning our experience you don't have to live it every day. Until you have to worry about your family making it home safe we don't want to hear nothing you have to say.

Letter to My Ancestors

This is for my ancestors I promise not to let you down for we were once royalty and I'll proudly strut my crown. You made your journey here in the bottom of a ship while so many others didn't survive the trip. Slaving in fields of cotton taking beatings for no reason until you mustered the strength to run for your freedom. The courage it took to run under the cover of dark not knowing what was to come on the journey you'd embark. Marching through the streets so that I could have rights segregated from places that were only for whites. Inheriting your spirit as a fighter it's because of you that I am a nurse and a writer. I'll never forget the price you paid for me and I will keep fighting to we're all fully free.

Black Woman in America

Being a black woman in America
we catch a lot of flack
treated as second class citizens
left to pick up the slack.
My black skin viewed as a weapon
for people to attack
oppressed over and over again in an
attempt to hold us back.
Constantly told that our thoughts, ideas,
and voices don't matter
so we try to assimilate and conform
to the master.
Not able to be our true selves
in public spaces
so we learn to juggle
so many different faces.
Then when we express how we feel

we get told we are angry
we're supposed to just take the disrespect
and stare at you blankly.
Trying to avoid the stereotype
so many of us hold back our yells
when we have a myriad of reasons
to be bitter and frankly mad as hell.
We're told this is the land of opportunity
but I'm not sure for who
because at the end of the day
we aren't given the same opportunities
as other races do.
No matter how many times we try to rise
we're at the bottom of the stack
I have two strikes against me I'm a woman
and I'm black.

www.ingramcontent.com/pod-product-compliance
Lightning Source LLC
LaVergne TN
LVHW020643100826
845148LV00012B/2309